CRITICALLY ENDANGERED: REPTILES

BOOK TWO

This book belongs to:

_____

This is an IndieMosh book
brought to you by MoshPit Publishing
an imprint of Mosher's Business Support Pty Ltd
PO Box 4363
Penrith NSW 2750
indiemosh.com.au

Copyright © Hannah Rowland 2021

The moral right of the author has been asserted in accordance with the Copyright Amendment (Moral Rights) Act 2000.

All rights reserved. Except as permitted under the Australian Copyright Act 1968 (for example, fair dealing for the purposes of study, research, criticism or review) no part of this publication may be reproduced, stored in a retrieval system, or transmitted in any form or by any means, electronic, mechanical, photocopying, recording or otherwise, without the written permission of the publisher.

A catalogue record for this work is available from the National Library of Australia

Title:	Conservation Collection AU - Critically Endangered
Subtitle:	Reptiles
Volume:	Book 2
Author:	Rowland, Hannah
Illustrator:	Corso, Sophie
ISBNs:	9781922628664 (paperback)
Subjects:	JUVENILE NONFICTION: Animals / Endangered; Science & Nature / Zoology; Science & Nature / Environmental Conservation & Protection; Concepts / Alphabet

The author has made every effort to ensure that the information in this book was correct at the time of publication. However, the author and publisher accept no liability for any loss, damage or disruption incurred by the reader or any other person arising from any action taken or not taken based on the content of this book. The author recommends seeking third party advice and considering all options prior to making any decision or taking action in regard to the content of this book.

Cover concept by Hannah Rowland
Cover and book layout by Ally Mosher (allymosher.com)

Conservation Collection AU established 2017

CONSERVATION COLLECTION AU

BOOK TWO

CRITICALLY ENDANGERED: REPTILES

Written by **Hannah Rowland** Illustrated by **Sophie Corso**

Introduction

Life on Earth has shown us the wondrous diversity of our Animal Kingdom. We have cute and cuddly mammals, amazing amphibians, bright and colourful feathered birds, creepy crawly invertebrates, fantastically adapted fish and slithering and scaly reptiles. Reptiles may not be as cute and cuddly as mammals, but they too must be protected from the threat of human impact on our planet.

Reptiles are fascinating creatures, in fact the earliest reptile fossil dates to approximately 315 million years ago. Since then, reptiles have grown in number to an estimated 11,500 known species.

Reptiles are a group of cold-blooded vertebrates (animals with backbones), distinguished from other animal groups by the presence of dry scaly skin or bony plates covering the body, and typically lay soft-shelled eggs. There are four classes of reptiles: Crocodilia (crocodiles, alligators, caiman and gharials), Sphenodontia (tuatara, a unique reptile native to New Zealand), Squamata (lizards, legless lizards, and snakes), and Testudines (turtles and tortoises). An estimated twenty percent of the world's reptiles are threatened with extinction. This book lists just twenty-six of those species that are CRITICALLY ENDANGERED.

The threats to most species in this series have evolved from human activity; cutting down the rainforests, creating roads and railways, and destroying the natural world around us are some of the main ways we have negatively impacted these creatures.

Many species have been hunted into extinction already; others—like those listed in this book—are close to extinction. It is the responsibility of humans to help fix what we can. We must help species that are critically endangered by conserving and preserving not only them, but their habitats as well.

These books have been written to inspire those future conservation crusaders and wildlife warriors to be advocates for Mother Nature. Many hours of research have gone into this book; many hours of looking at specific species and their habitats, and how they are threatened. It is our wish that this book inspires you to work together to help some of the following species so that one day they are no longer on the endangered list.

Scale and definitions: IUCN 2019. *The IUCN Red List of Threatened Species. Version 2019-3.* http://www.iucnredlist.org.

What does it mean to be "Critically Endangered"?

Below: Red List categories by the International Union for Conservation of Nature (IUCN)

NE	NOT EVALUATED
DD	DATA DEFICIENT
LC	LEAST CONCERN
NT	NEAR THREATENED
VU	VULNERABLE
EN	ENDANGERED
CR	CRITICALLY ENDANGERED
EW	EXTINCT IN THE WILD
EX	EXTINCT

The author and contributors would like to note that although species featured have been evaluated as 'Critically Endangered', the status of these species may be updated as new information is discovered.

The IUCN definition of 'Critically Endangered' is as follows:

'A species facing extremely high risk of extinction in the wild'

Species must meet criteria upon assessment by the IUCN Species Survival Commission, Red List Authorities or Red List Partners to be correctly categorised on the IUCN List.

Least Concern: A species of Least Concern has been evaluated and does not meet the criteria for Near Threatened, Vulnerable, Endangered or Critically Endangered statuses. Often these species are common and numerous.

Near Threatened: A species is Near Threatened when its evaluation does not meet the criteria for Vulnerable, Endangered or Critically Endangered status, but is likely to qualify for a threatened status in the near future.

Vulnerable: A species is Vulnerable when the best available records or supportive evidence indicates that it is facing high risk of extinction, but does not meet the criteria for Endangered status. Particular criteria must be met to be categorised in this status.

Endangered: A species is Endangered when the best available records or supportive evidence indicates that it is facing very high (but not extreme) risk of extinction in the wild. Particular criteria must be met to be categorised in this status.

Critically Endangered: A species is Critically Endangered when the best available records or supportive evidence indicates that it is facing extremely high risk of extinction in the wild. Particular criteria must be met to be categorised in this status.

Extinct In The Wild: A species is Extinct In The Wild when it is known only to survive in captivity, and/or as a natural population well outside the past range.

Extinct: A species is Extinct when there is no reasonable doubt that the last individual has died. A species may be declared Extinct when exhaustive surveys in the known or expected habitat have failed to record an individual over a time period.

Big Words to Learn!

Annual
The term 'annual' refers to crops grown by farmers that complete their entire life cycle within one growing season and must be replanted each year.

Artificial
In this book, 'artificial' describes animals' habitats that are man-made or not naturally occurring in their geographical region (including non-native forests).

Clutch
A group of eggs produced at the same time by the female reptile, especially those laid in a nest.

Endemic
Native to, and restricted to, a particular geographical region.

Gene flow
The transfer of genes from one population to another to create a new or varied gene pool.

Genera
The plural form of Genus (see below).

Genus
A group of related living things (animals or plants) that rank below the family in taxonomic classification and is made up of one or more species. For example, classification of a domestic dog looks like:

Family *Canidae*, Genus *Canis*, Species *Canis lupus*, Subspecies *Canis lupus familiaris*.

Geographical region
In this book, 'geographical region' refers to the physical land area that an animal habitat may occur or be created in.

Habitat
A habitat is the place where the animal lives and is able to find food, water, and shelter.

Herpetologist/Herpetology
A 'herpetologist' is a person specialising in the care and handling of reptiles and amphibians. 'Herpetology' is the study of reptiles and amphibians.

Incubated/Incubation
The process by which egg-laying reptiles hatch their eggs; including the development of the young reptile inside the egg under favourable environmental condition. Most reptiles lay eggs that hatch outside the female's body in a nest (for example, turtles and tortoises). Favourable environmental conditions for nest-laid eggs means that the temperature is suitable (not too cold), the nest material is suitable (leaves, sand, or soil) and the nest area is protected from predators and weather. Some reptiles keep their eggs inside their body until the young are ready to hatch and give birth to their young in a similar way to mammals.

Intertidal
The area of a seashore that is covered at high tide and uncovered at low tide.

Invasive species
Invasive species describes species that are not native to the area where they are found. This means that the plant or animal has found its way out of its native habitat and into a new area. An example of an invasive species in Australia is the European rabbit.

Perennial
The term 'perennial' refers to crops grown by farmers that do not have to be replanted every year, and instead continue to regrow after harvesting.

Pigment
A 'pigment' is a substance that gives something a particular colour.

Population fragmentation
'Population fragmentation' occurs when groups of animals living in the wild become separated from other groups of the same species, and are no longer connected in a way that allows for gene flow between groups.

Repatriate
Releasing individuals of a particular species into an area formally or currently occupied by that species.

Repopulate/Repopulation
In conservation, this is defined as a planned release of a particular species into the natural habitat, of specimens of the same wild subspecies or, in the event the existence of subspecies had not been determined, of the same wild species, for the purpose of strengthening a reduced population.

Specimen
Any living or dead animal or plant.

Subspecies
A group within a species that has become somewhat physically and genetically different from the rest of the group. A 'subspecies' is still capable of breeding within the rest of the species.

Taxonomic group/ classification
The classification system used to group living things. The major groups commonly used are Kingdom, Phylum, Class, Order, Family, Genus, Species.

Terrestrial
Land-based ecosystem. In this book, 'terrestrial' describes the animal living on or near the ground.

Zoological
Relating to the study of animals. A 'zoo' is the shortened form of 'zoological'.

For Loz, whose love for all creatures great and small—especially reptiles and amphibians—lives on in the species she helped save. You will always be our wildlife warrior.

The author and contributors would like to reiterate that although species featured have been evaluated as 'Critically Endangered', the status of these species may be updated as new information is discovered and species are reassessed.

The International Union for Conservation of Nature (IUCN) definition of 'Critically Endangered' is as follows:

'A species facing extremely high risk of extinction in the wild.'

Species must meet criteria upon assessment by the IUCN Species Survival Commission, Red List Authorities, or Red List Partners to be correctly categorised on the IUCN list.

CRITICALLY ENDANGERED: REPTILES

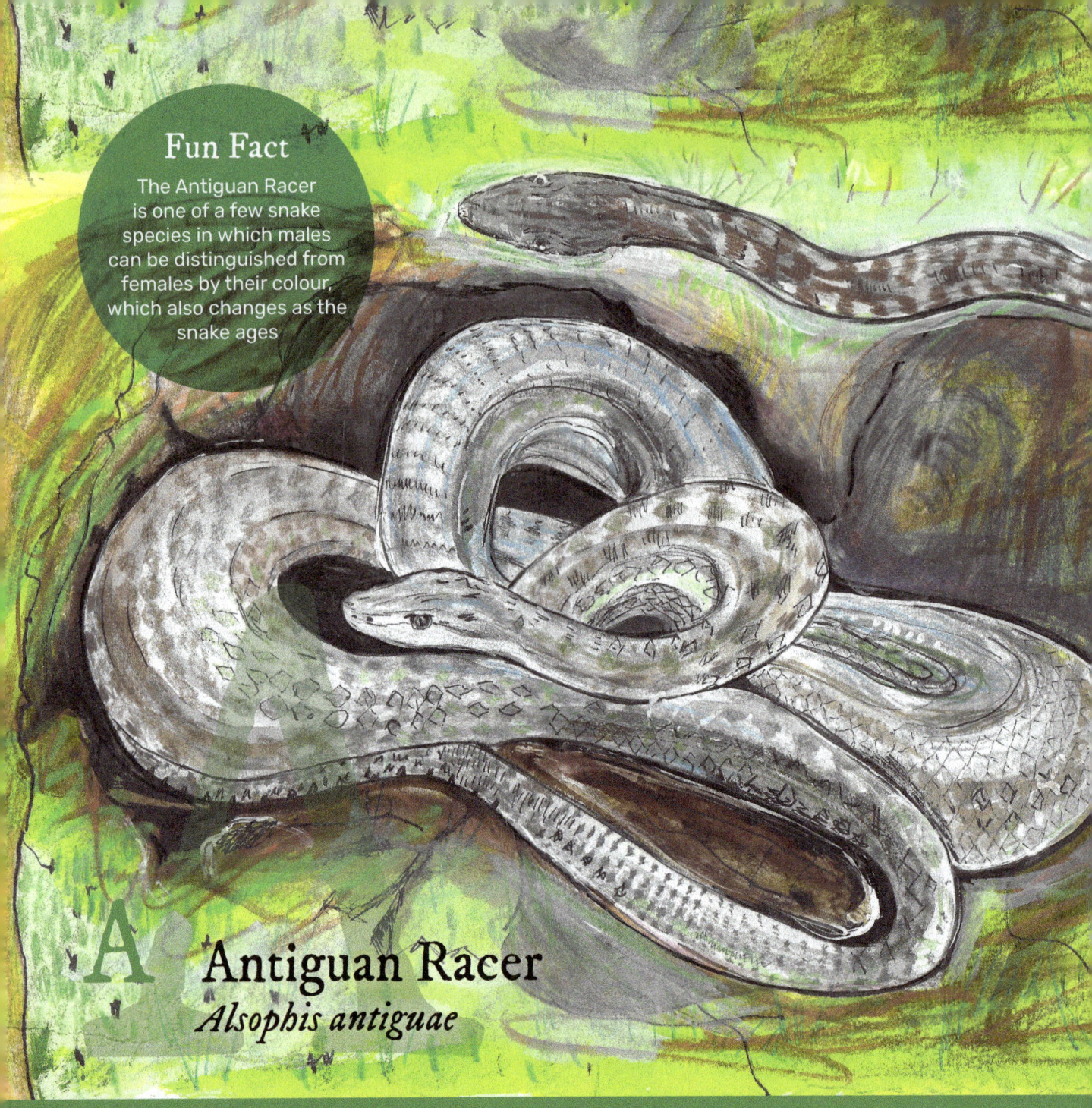

> **Fun Fact**
> The Antiguan Racer is one of a few snake species in which males can be distinguished from females by their colour, which also changes as the snake ages

Antiguan Racer
Alsophis antiguae

Status: Critically Endangered
Population: Estimated 1100
Found: Antigua, Barbuda
Habitat Type: Forest
Threats: Invasive species and diseases, natural disaster (fire/flood), human activity

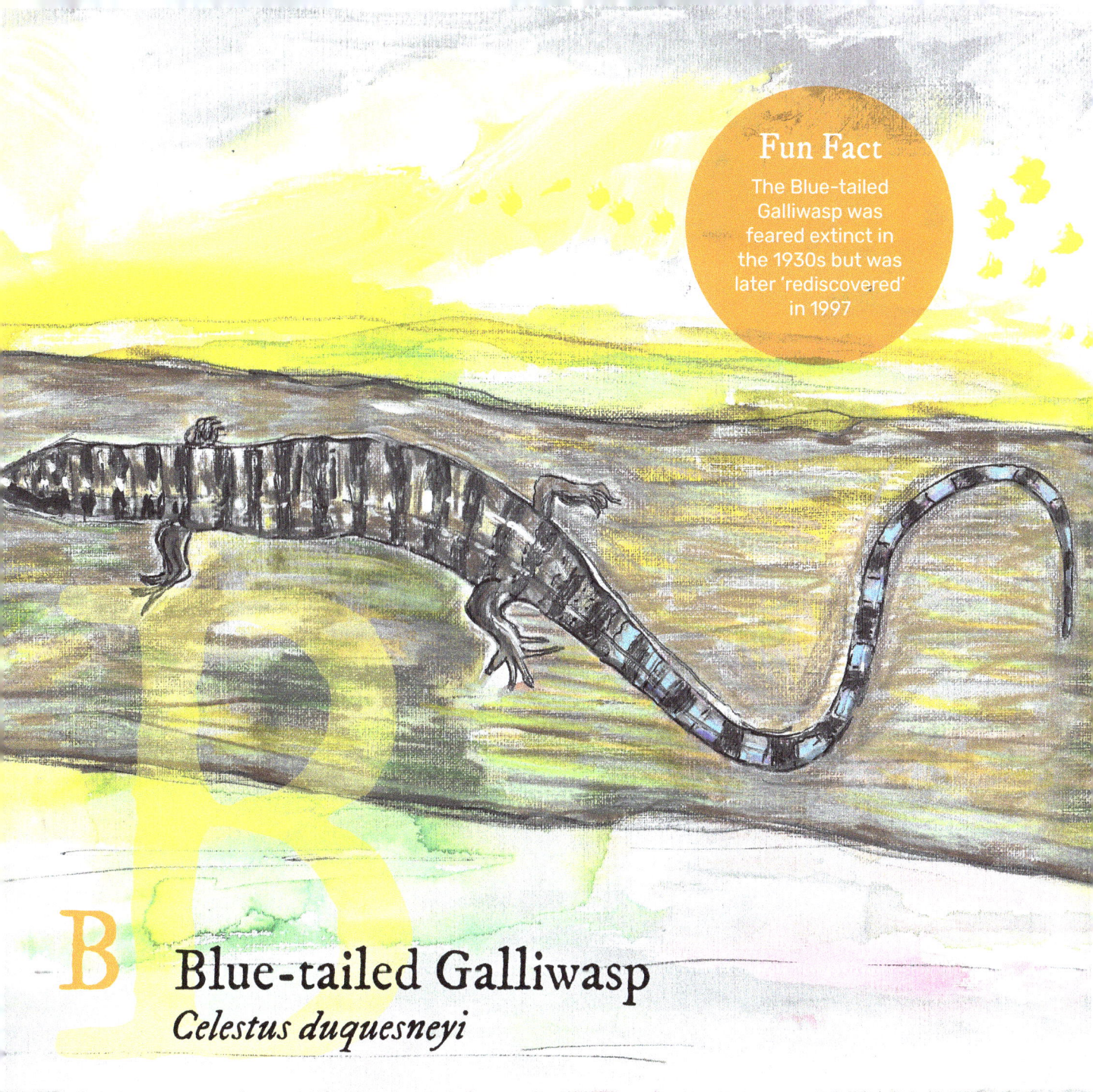

Fun Fact
The Blue-tailed Galliwasp was feared extinct in the 1930s but was later 'rediscovered' in 1997

Blue-tailed Galliwasp
Celestus duquesneyi

Status: Critically Endangered
Population: Population Unknown—In Decline
Found: Jamaica
Habitat Type: Forest
Threats: Invasive species and diseases, logging and wood harvesting, commercial and industrial development

Fun Fact
Campbell's Alligator Lizard was only described as a new species in 1993. It was presumed extinct a short time after this until its 'rediscovery' in 2010

Campbell's Alligator Lizard
Abronia campbelli

Status: Critically Endangered
Population: 500
Found: Guatemala
Habitat Type: Forest
Threats: Livestock farming, hunting and trapping, pollution (agriculture and forestry)

Durban Dwarf Burrowing Skink
Scelotes inornatus

Fun Fact
Durban Dwarf Burrowing Skinks do not have legs, but they are not a type of snake. They are completely harmless, feeding off ground-dwelling insects

Status: Critically Endangered
Population: Unknown—In Decline
Found: Durban, South Africa
Habitat Type: Forest
Threats: Invasive species and diseases, agriculture, housing and urbanisation, commercial development, and transport infrastructure

El Hierro Giant Lizard
Gallotia simonyi

Fun Fact
Female El Hierro Giant Lizards will lay 6–12 eggs per clutch, which are incubated for roughly 61 days before hatching

Status: Critically Endangered
Population: Last estimated at 300–400
Found: Spain
Habitat Type: Shrubland, rocky areas
Threats: Hunting and trapping, invasive species, and diseases

Flat-tailed Tortoise
Pyxis planicauda

Fun Fact

Males of this species may weigh between 300–400 grams, while females are slightly larger weighing between 475–670 grams

Status: Critically Endangered
Population: Last estimated less than 10,000
Found: Madagascar
Habitat Type: Forest
Threats: Hunting and trapping, logging and wood harvesting, roads and railways, livestock farming and ranching, mining, fire, and fire suppression

Fun Fact
The pink colouration of their skin is due to lack of pigment, making the blood underneath visible

G Galápagos Pink Iguana
Conolophus marthae

Status: Critically Endangered
Population: Last estimated 192 adult individuals
Found: Wolf Volcano, Isabela Island (Galapagos)
Habitat Type: Shrubland, forest
Threats: Invasive species and diseases, drought, volcanoes

Hawksbill Sea Turtle
Eretmochelys imbricata

Fun Fact
Hawksbill Sea Turtles get their name from the sharp, curved shape of their beak, which resembles that of a bird of prey. They use this beak to feed on sea sponges, molluscs, algae, and sea worms

Status: Critically Endangered
Population: Estimated 20,000–23,000 nesting females
Found: Atlantic Ocean, Indian Ocean, Pacific Ocean
Habitat Type: Marine
Threats: Pollution, tourism and recreational activities, oil and gas drilling, fishing and harvesting of aquatic resources, climate change and severe weather events

> **Fun Fact**
> The bottom part of the Indochinese Box Turtle's shell (called the plastron) is 'hinged', allowing the turtle to completely seal itself within their shell to protect themselves from predators

1 Indochinese Box Turtle
Cuora galbinifrons

Status: Critically Endangered
Population: Estimated less than 10,000–40,000
Found: China, Laos, Vietnam
Habitat Type: Forest
Threats: Hunting and trapping, livestock farming and ranching, wood and pulp plantations, annual and perennial non-timber crops, mining and quarrying, dams and water management systems

Jeypore Ground Gecko
Geckoella jeyporensis, Cyrtodactylus jeyporensis

Fun Fact
The Jeypore Ground Gecko was thought to be extinct until 2010, when members of a research team discovered a young adult male. In 2011, another adult male was found

Status: Critically Endangered
Population: Unknown
Found: India
Habitat Type: Forest
Threats: Logging and wood harvesting, wood and pulp plantations, fire and fire suppression, mining and quarrying, livestock farming

Fun Fact

Kemp's Ridley Sea Turtle are the smallest of the seven sea turtle species. They also nest primarily during the day, unlike other species

K Kemp's Ridley Sea Turtle
Lepidochelys kempii

Status: Critically Endangered
Population: Estimated 22,341 adult individuals
Found: Atlantic Ocean
Habitat Type: Marine
Threats: Oil and gas drilling, fishing and harvesting of aquatic resources

> **Fun Fact**
> As an air-breathing species, the Leaf-scaled Sea Snake must come to the surface every 30–120 minutes between each dive in order to take a breath

L Leaf-scaled Sea Snake
Aipysurus foliosquama

Status: Critically Endangered
Population: Current population estimate may be less than 100
Found: Shark Bay and Ashmore Reef, Western Australia
Habitat Type: Marine
Threats: Habitat shifting and alteration, offshore development activities

Fun Fact
The Magdalena River Turtle is found only in the Magdalena and Sinu Rivers of Colombia

M Magdalena River Turtle
Podocnemis lewyana

Status: Critically Endangered
Population: Unknown—Reportedly declining by 8.8% each year
Found: Colombia
Habitat Type: Wetlands (freshwater inlands)
Threats: Livestock farming and ranching, fishing and harvesting aquatic resources, damming, water management and use

Fun Fact

Nevin's Three-toed Slider was named after Anne Nevin, a staff member of the Natural Sciences Department in the Western Australian Museum between 1982 and 2006

Nevin's Three-toed Slider
Lerista nevinae

Status: Critically Endangered
Population: Unknown due to population fragmentation
Found: Western Australia (Endemic between Dickson Island and Point Samson)
Habitat Type: Marine coastal, and shrubland
Threats: Tourism and recreation areas, recreational activities, mining and quarrying, logging and wood harvesting, invasive species and diseases

Fun Fact
The Orinoco Crocodile is South America's largest crocodilian species

Orinoco Crocodile
Crocodylus intermedius

Status: Critically Endangered
Population: Estimated less than 250
Found: Bolivia, Colombia, Venezuela
Habitat Type: Forest, savanna, wetlands (freshwater inlands)
Threats: Fishing and harvesting aquatic resources, annual and perennial non-timber crops, livestock farming and ranching

Philippine Crocodile
Crocodylus mindorensis

Fun Fact: While only female Philippine Crocodiles build the nest for their eggs, both the male and the female will guard it

Status: Critically Endangered
Population: Less than 150
Found: Dalupiri Island and Ligawasan Marsh, Philippines
Habitat Type: Wetlands (inland)
Threats: Annual and perennial non-timber crops, fishing and harvesting of aquatic resources

Fun Fact
The Queretaran Desert Lizard is a member of the genus Sceloporus, a group of small iguana-like lizards, native to North and Central America

Queretaran Desert Lizard
Sceloporus exsul

Status: Critically Endangered
Population: Unknown (in decline)
Found: Mexico
Habitat Type: Shrubland
Threats: Livestock farming and ranching, mining and quarrying

> **Fun Fact**
> Rabino's Tree Iguana was thought extinct in the mid-1970's until it was rediscovered in 2010

Rabino's Tree Iguana
Liolaemus rabinoi

Status: Critically Endangered
Population: A group of 18–20 individuals were discovered in 2010, however the species is in continuous decline
Found: Argentina
Habitat Type: Desert
Threats: Energy production (including renewable energy), human recreational activities

> **Fun Fact**
> A total of 1033 Santiago Giant Tortoises were repatriated to Santiago Island from the Santa Cruz Fausto Llerena Breeding Centre between 1975 and 2014 to help repopulate the species

Santiago Giant Tortoise
Chelonoidis darwini

Status: Critically Endangered
Population: 500–1700
Found: Santiago Island (Galapagos Islands)
Habitat Type: Forest, shrubland
Threats: Hunting and trapping of terrestrial animals, invasive species and diseases

Toyama Ground Gecko
Goniurosaurus toyami

Fun Fact
The genus *Goniurosaurus* that Toyama's Ground Gecko is part of, split from other lizards prior to the extinction of the dinosaurs

Status: Critically Endangered
Population: Unknown—Population is endemic and in continuous decline
Found: Iheyajima Island, Japan
Habitat Type: Forest
Threats: Roads and railways, dams and water management, hunting and trapping of terrestrial animals

Fun Fact
Utila Spiny-tailed Iguanas will avoid predators by entering the water near mangrove roots and swimming or diving beneath the surface

Utila Spiny-tailed Iguana
Ctenosaura bakeri

Status: Critically Endangered
Population: Less than 6000
Found: Utila Island (Honduras)
Habitat Type: Forest, grassland, marine intertidal
Threats: Residential and commercial development, tourism and recreation areas, roads and railways, annual and perennial non-timber crops, pollution, climate change and severe weather, invasive species and diseases

Viper (Darevsky's)
Vipera darevskii

Fun Fact
Darevsky's Viper was named after the Russian herpetologist Ilya S. Darevsky (1924–2009) who collected the first specimen

Status: Critically Endangered
Population: Estimated less than 1000
Found: Armenia, Turkey
Habitat Type: Rocky areas (inland cliffs and mountain peaks)
Threats: Livestock farming and ranching

Fun Fact
Wagner's Viper was thought extinct for nearly 140 years before being 'rediscovered' in 1983

Wagner's Viper
Montivipera wagneri

Status: Critically Endangered
Population: Unclear—While numbers are in decline in the wild, conservation programs in zoological facilities have successfully bred a small number of Wagner's Vipers
Found: Turkey
Habitat Type: Rocky areas (inland cliffs and mountain peaks)
Threats: Hunting and trapping terrestrial animals, dams and water management

Fun Fact
The Madagascar Blind Snake uses its head to burrow through the sandy soil it lives in

Xenotyphlops grandidieri
Madagascar Blind Snake

Status: Critically Endangered
Population: Unknown—reported as in decline due to habitat destruction
Found: Madagascar
Habitat Type: Forest, shrubland, marine coastal
Threats: Mining and quarrying, logging and wood harvesting

Fun Fact
The total area that Yamashina's Ground Geckoes are found in is just 60 km²; an area so tiny it could fit 128,000 times into the size of Australia

Yamashina's Ground Gecko
Goniurosaurus yamashinae

Status: Critically Endangered
Population: Unknown due to population fragmentation. Population in decline
Found: Kumejima Island, Japan
Habitat Type: Forest (artificial and terrestrial)
Threats: Annual and perennial non-timber crops, roads and railways, hunting and trapping of terrestrial animals

Fun Fact
Odd-scaled Snakes are so-called because their scales do not overlap like most snakes, but instead are spread out and lie individually

Z Zong's Odd-scaled Snake
Achalinus jinggangensis

Status: Critically Endangered
Population: Comprehensive studies conducted over 2010 and 2011 found only 5 individuals concluding that the wild population is decreasing and likely a small number
Found: China
Habitat Type: Forest
Threats: Housing and urban development, mining and quarrying

Bibliography

All biographic information has been sourced from the International Union for Conservation of Nature (IUCN) Red List of Threatened Species:

https://www.iucnredlist.org

Additional biographic information and introduction supporting information:

https://www.nationalgeographic.com/animals/reptiles

https://wwf.panda.org/discover/knowledge_hub/endangered_species/marine_turtles/

http://www.reptile-database.org/db-info/SpeciesStat.html

'Fun Facts' bibliography:

https://buffalozoo.org/animal/indochinese-box-turtle/

https://www.cuora.org/cuora-galbinifrons

https://www.edgeofexistence.org

https://www.fauna-flora.org/species/antiguan-racer

https://galapagosconservation.org.uk/wildlife/galapagos-pink-land-iguana/

https://www.hoglezoo.org/meet_our_animals/animal_finder/madagascan_flat-tailed_tortoise/

https://www.inaturalist.org/taxa/27576-Achalinus

https://www.marwell.org.uk/zoo/explore/animals/109/utila-spiny-tailed-iguana

https://nationalzoo.si.edu/animals/philippine-crocodile

https://oceana.org/marine-life/sea-turtles-reptiles/hawksbill-turtle

https://reptile-database.reptarium.cz/species?genus=Gallotia&species=simonyi

https://savegoatislands.org/photos-videos/reptiles-amphibians/

https://www.seaturtle-world.com/sea-turtle-feeding/

https://www.seeturtles.org/sea-turtle-diet

https://southlandssun.co.za/32846/gods-littlecreatures-durban-dwarf-burrowing-skink/

https://www.stlzoo.org/animals/abouttheanimals/reptiles/snakes/ocellatemountainviper

https://taronga.org.au/news/2018-07-11/tarongas-support-alligator-lizard-conservation-update-guatemala

https://www.turtleconservancy.org/turtles-in-trouble

https://www.worldlandtrust.org/species/reptiles/magdalena-river-turtle/

About the Author

Hannah is based in New South Wales, Australia and has had years of experience with animals both endangered and domestic species, which has inspired her to produce a book for children to assist in educating about such conservation topics. Hannah's special interest has been to highlight species that may not be commonly recognised due to their critically endangered status or less-cuddly appearances.

Hannah is qualified in Natural Science (Animal Science, Conservation Biology, Zoology) and her collaborative team are members of the veterinary, wildlife, and environmental conservation fields.

Hannah and her team have worked carefully in their research to be sure that all information is up to date and correct with the current International Union for Conservation of Nature (IUCN) Red List of Threatened Species. Despite this, the declining population rate of some species listed in this book at the time of publication will mean these species may already be extinct, however the hope is that some populations will increase.

The Conservation Collection Au Project was founded in 2017 and continues to develop its program.

About the Illustrator

Illustrator Sophie Corso is an Adelaide-based artist with Honours in Visual Art from the University of South Australia. Sophie has previously illustrated animal characters for *A Ferret Named Phil and The Old Ferris Wheel* (written by William Reimer).

Mission Statement

Founded in 2017, our mission statement "Care for Conservation - Their Future is In Our Hands" is about creating a fun educational program known as the Conservation Collection (Au) to learn about endangered animals and their habitats.

We promote a message of conservation and preservation of the Earth's species, both flora and fauna, from the little contributions at home to the global team efforts of many organisations.

Our current project is taking ground, developing a program for children including up-to-date easy-reader books and learning activities about critically endangered species and their habitats. With support, this project aims to inspire the next generation of conservation crusaders to carry on the legacy of caring for Earth's most endangered species.

www.ingramcontent.com/pod-product-compliance
Lightning Source LLC
LaVergne TN
LVHW070207080526
838202LV00063B/6572